Elizabeth of the Trinity

by
Jennifer Moorcroft

*All booklets are published thanks to the
generous support of the members of the
Catholic Truth Society*

CATHOLIC TRUTH SOCIETY

PUBLISHERS TO THE HOLY SEE

Contents

Introduction 3

Life in the World 5

Into the Land of Carmel. 18

The Praise of Glory 28

The Fellowship of his Sufferings. 38

From the Writings of
Saint Elizabeth of the Trinity. 48

Suggested Further Reading 61

Images: Pages 4, 9, 16 and 23: Willuconquer, Wikimedia Commons.

ISBN 978 1 78469 148 6

Introduction

With her canonisation on 16th October 2016, Elizabeth of the Trinity became the fourth great Carmelite saint, together with St John of the Cross, St Teresa of Avila and St Thérèse of Lisieux, who are the outstanding teachers of prayer in the Catholic Church.

Today, many people are searching for greater depth in their lives and often going to Eastern religions and meditation techniques for inspiration. St Elizabeth of the Trinity reminds us of the immense riches we have in the Catholic faith to guide us in the paths of prayer and union with God. She herself drew above all on the Scriptures, and especially on her "beloved St Paul" for inspiration; so intensively did she live his teachings and those of St John, that they became not simply and inspiration, but the very expression of her own inner life.

She lived only five years in Carmel, but twenty-one as a lay person, and had already attained a degree of holiness before entering the cloister. In Carmel she saw no contradiction between what she lived as a religious and what was also possible for a lay person: all are called to holiness and union with God. St Teresa of Avila said we could find God in the midst of pots and pans, and Elizabeth echoed this when she said "we find God at the wash just as at prayer".

4

A happy Carmelite

Elizabeth's Prioress, Mother Germaine of Jesus, called her "a happy Carmelite" and this joy permeated her whole life even in the midst of the atrocious sufferings in her final months. Because she lived in love and her horizon was the infinity of God, she had an expansiveness of soul that reminds us that the Christian should be the most joyous of people.

St Elizabeth's reputation as one of the most influential mystics of the twentieth century has been steadily growing since her death in 1906; it is to be hoped that more people will be drawn to her as a sure guide in the way of prayer and the path of holiness, and will be inspired by the beauty of her personality as expressed in her writings and example.

Life in the World

On 18th July 1880 Captain Joseph Catez hurried across the French army camp at Avord, near Bourges, to the chaplain's house. His wife Marie was in labour with their first child and was dangerously ill; both her life and the baby's life were in danger. There was cause for concern, because Marie and Joseph had married late and had never expected to have children. Joseph was now forty-eight and Marie was thirty-four, so could M. l'Abbé offer Mass for them that all would be well? The chaplain did so, and as he finished Mass Elizabeth Catez came safely into the world. Two years later Elizabeth, nicknamed Sabeth, was joined by a sister, Marguerite, always known as Guite, and the Catez family was complete.

In those first years, Captain and Madame Catez had good reason to feel anything but blessed in their elder daughter. Whereas Marguerite had a loving and gentle character, Elizabeth, a real chatterbox, had inherited all the fire and spirit of her parents' military background. She had a quick temper and a will of iron. The slightest opposition would send her into a tantrum, and all her mother could do was to lock her into a room where she would scream and kick the furniture until she had calmed down. With good reason she was called the little captain. She showed this imperiousness when her mother took Elizabeth to visit her elderly parents in Saint-Hilaire. A mission was being held there, ending with a special service of blessing for the children. One of the sisters organising it came to ask for the loan of Elizabeth's favourite doll, Jeanette, to stand in for the baby Jesus. Unfortunately Elizabeth recognised her doll, and to the amusement of the congregation, her eyes blazing, loudly demanded back her doll.

Nevertheless, even at an early age, and in that devout household, her parents noted that she had a genuine love for Jesus and was quiet and prayerful when in church.

First Confession and First Holy Communion

In 1886 Captain Catez retired from the army, having been diagnosed with a heart condition, and the family moved to Dijon; in the following year first Elizabeth's beloved grandfather died and, later in the year, her father died also. It made a great difference to the family's circumstances, because Madame Catez now had only a service pension to live on; they rented the upstairs floor of a house owned by a M. Chapuis, just around the corner from the Carmelite monastery.

It was a crucial time for Elizabeth; she made her first Confession around Christmas 1887, in preparation for her First Communion in five years' time. During this period, visiting Canon Angles, a close family friend, Elizabeth climbed on to his lap and whispered, "I am going to be a nun; I will be a nun!" Her mother overheard, and despite having considered a religious vocation herself when she was younger, she was horrified, but hoped that it was just a childish fancy. From the age of seven her mother began to take her regularly to Sunday Mass, and the Eucharist remained at the heart of her spiritual life.

Having made her Confession, and realising perhaps the effect her tantrums were having on her beloved mother, Elizabeth began to make heroic efforts to control her temper. Also, Mme Catez had threatened to postpone the date of her First Communion if she didn't improve. She used her iron will against herself, as it were, but she was also motivated by an ever deepening love for Jesus. It was a real battle in the small things of a child's life. One friend remembered seeing tears in her eyes as she gave way in deciding what game they should play. Her parish priest declared that she would become either a saint or a demon and at one point he tried to control her high spirits by making her kneel in the road.

Both the girls were highly gifted musically and Mme Catez enrolled them in the Dijon Conservatoire to study piano. It was judged that while Guite had more technical skill, Elizabeth played with more sensitivity and depth. Elizabeth was becoming increasingly calm and gentle and found that in music she could express her love for Jesus beyond words.

Elizabeth made her First Communion on 19th April 1891 at the age of twelve, declaring it to be the most beautiful day of her life. In the afternoon Elizabeth went with her mother to the Carmelite monastery to meet the Prioress, Mother Mary of Jesus, who gave her a small card with a picture and a verse on it, which gave the meaning of her name, Elizabeth: the house of God, the dwelling place of the Trinity.[1] She was confirmed on 8th June 1891.

Determination to be a nun

As she passed into her teens her mother could not help but realise that her daughter's determination to be a nun was no passing fancy. She may not have known that Elizabeth had made a private vow of virginity when she was fourteen, but her frequent visits to Carmel forced Mme Catez to realise that her daughter's thoughts were turning more and more to the cloister. At Mass one day, Elizabeth had heard within herself the call to Carmel, and from her bedroom window she could see the grounds of the Carmel and the nuns there going about their work and prayer. Her mother, on the other hand, was determined that Elizabeth should look elsewhere for her future, perhaps as a music teacher.

Elizabeth left the Conservatoire at the age of sixteen. Due to Conservatoire "politics", she was deprived of the Award for Excellence that should have been hers, but Guite won it two years later. Because their general education was not keeping up with their musical studies, Mme Catez engaged

Elizabeth as a young child playing the piano

a tutor, Mlle Forey. In order to know the girls better, she gave them an essay to write, to describe their physical and moral portrait. Elizabeth was not exactly complimentary about her physical appearance, and for her moral character, without revealing her inner spiritual life, wrote:

> I would say that I have rather a good character. I am cheerful and, I must confess, somewhat scatter-brained. I have a good heart. I am by nature a coquette; Some say "one should be somewhat". I am not lazy: I know that "work makes us happy". Without being a model of patience, I usually know how to control myself. I do not hold grudges. So much for my moral portrait. I have my defects and, alas, few good qualities! I hope to acquire them![2]

There was a very deep bond between Mme Catez and her daughters, they dubbed themselves "the three", and Mme Catez could not bear the thought of Elizabeth shut away from her forever in a convent. Elizabeth was growing into a lovely girl, graceful, simple and elegant, with a charm and vivacity that endeared her to everyone. Her mother wanted her to meet some suitable young army officer, perhaps, for whom she would make an excellent wife, and she felt sure that soon there would be no lack of offers. The idea of her becoming a nun was unthinkable.

Call to Carmel

When, at the age of sixteen Elizabeth told her mother of her call to Carmel, to her great distress, her mother refused her permission to visit the Carmel or speak to the nuns. In order to distract Elizabeth, her mother launched her into a round of visits to relatives, parties, country trips, balls and military reviews that formed the principal occupations of young girls of her class at that time. Despite their relative poverty and the loss of status from being a military wife, they had loyal friends who discreetly helped them out financially by inviting them to their houses, especially during the summer months. This was no sacrifice on their part, because the two girls, and their mother made delightful guests. Elizabeth loved the times they stayed with the "Rolland aunts", her mother's sisters, at Carlipa, "that little corner of heaven", a tiny village with a backdrop of the Pyrenees, where she could walk in the tranquillity of the evening. She was equally enthralled by the scenery of Luchon, when they took a landau to the "Gulf of Hell", high up in the mountains. To the terror of the rest of the party, Elizabeth and her friend Madeleine pranced around the edge of the awesome ravine, completely unaffected by the enormous drop plunging to the waters below. It was at Carlipa that Elizabeth probably began writing her diary. She also began writing poems which helped her put into words her spiritual journey, especially after she entered Carmel.

With their musical accomplishments, Elizabeth and Guite were often called upon to play the piano at dances and soirées. As Elizabeth wrote to a friend, Alice:

> Our stay here has been a round of pleasures; dancing matinées, musical matinées, country expeditions, one thing after another… We hardly leave the piano, and the music shops in Tarbes can scarcely provide us with enough to play on sight.[3]

The girls had a wide circle of friends, and so she was writing to Alice again:

> We are having a really delightful time at Luneville, lunching with these and dining with those, as well as frequent tennis parties with some lovely girls; in a word, we don't have a minute to ourselves and don't know where we are.[4]

In all these visits and times with friends Elizabeth was most appreciated not only for her kindness and thoughtfulness, but also for her tremendous drive and sense of fun. Her friend Françoise summed her up at this time: "She did not love the world but she was in it and seemed to enjoy herself."

Parish activities and longing for solitude

When Elizabeth was at home she was very much involved in parish activities. She especially enjoyed helping with children, teaching the catechism and helping to run a youth club for the working-class children of the parish. She was a gifted story-teller, able to keep them enthralled for hours, and was so popular with them that she had to conceal her address from them to prevent her house from being invaded at all hours.

Nevertheless, all this activity did not prevent her from longing for Carmel and the silence she would find there. At this time, her mother became seriously ill due to a snake bite and Elizabeth was faced with the prospect of never being able to enter Carmel, but instead looking after her mother. So she purposed to become a "Carmelite in the world"; the realisation that the Carmelite charism of apostolic prayer could be lived in the world later helped her, when in Carmel, to counsel her friends in following the interior life of prayer that was open to all. She took for her own St Catherine of Siena's teaching of having an "inner cell" in which she prayed to her Master, as she loved to call Jesus, wherever she was.

Nevertheless, her inner struggle was affecting her health, and this was brought to a head during a parish mission of 1899. Elizabeth kept a diary of this time which is still extant. Her sister Guite realised how deeply Elizabeth was affected by their mother's continued opposition, and despite her own anguish at the thought of losing her sister to the cloister, she went to Mme Catez to plead her sister's cause. When her mother realised that Elizabeth's health and happiness were at stake she agreed, heartbroken, to allow her to enter - but not before she was twenty-one. That was still three years away, Mme Catez thought to herself, and anything could happen in the meantime…

Overjoyed as she was at her mother's agreement, Elizabeth was heartbroken to see the suffering of the two she loved most on earth, with all three in tears. But the call of Jesus was too strong for her to resist. That evening, she wrote in her diary:

> I would do anything to spare them the slightest pain, and it is I who am causing them so much suffering. And yet, Master, I know you want me and you are giving me the strength and courage I need; in my pain I feel a deep, deep peace and calm. Yes, I will soon be answering your call. During these two years I want to try even harder to be a bride less unworthy of you, my Beloved.[5]

Finding a spiritual director

Mme Catez now allowed Elizabeth to visit the Carmel again, where she made many new friends. The Dijon Carmel at that time was full up and preparing to make a foundation in Paray-le-Monial under Mother Mary of Jesus; Elizabeth joined a group of young women hoping to enter Carmel. The Prioress called this group her "postulants outside the walls". They came to her for spiritual guidance and helped the sisters with tasks in the sacristy and chapel. Elizabeth was also fortunate to meet a priest on her visits to Carmel, Fr Vallée, who became her spiritual director. She wanted his advice, because new things were developing in her spiritual life that she wanted to understand.

"It feels", she said to a friend, "as if Someone is within me, as if I were dwelt in." During her times of prayer Elizabeth seemed to be able to do less and less for herself. Fr Vallée helped her to understand that she was truly a "house of God", in whom dwelt the Trinity, in the words of St Paul, "Do you not understand that you are God's temple, and that God's spirit is dwelling in you?" Her inner cell contained a Divine Guest.

She was also reading the newly published autobiography of St Thérèse of Lisieux, and wrote her own act of surrender to God. In another prayer she said she wanted to be a saint, to give her heart wholly to him, to do only his will: she offered to him "the cell of my heart to be your little Bethany; come and live there, I love you so much".

Not for us

Elizabeth was soon to be twenty-one. Then one day Mme Catez came home in great excitement; she had received an offer for Elizabeth's hand from a most eligible officer; surely she would not dream of refusing! Elizabeth did refuse, and firmly, and her mother had to bow to the inevitable. Young men at a soirée more discerning than this officer, who saw her beauty, her charm and vivacity, saw also a look in her eyes that took her far from the gaiety of the evening, and knew "she was not for us".

Elizabeth, aged 20

The date for her entry was fixed for 2nd August 1901, but there was one problem. Mother Mary of Jesus had decided that Elizabeth should enter the new foundation at Paray-le-Monial, which had been founded on 30th June 1901, and her bags had already been packed and sent on ahead. However, her mother was seriously worried about the effect such hardships would have on her daughter's health and wrote to Mother Mary of Jesus expressing her worries. The prioress immediately wrote to Elizabeth herself:

> You are no doubt aware that your mother and Marguerite have asked to let you stay in Dijon; it seems that this is also what you would prefer. I see in all this the will of the good God which we should love and do without a second thought. Give yourself to the Lord wherever he wills; I don't want you here if it isn't what he wants. So I shall receive you for Dijon, my dear child; bring all that you have of heart and soul to love our Lord.[6]

Elizabeth herself was ready to accept all the hardships and privations of the new Carmel, but her heart had really been set on Dijon. Now, God's will could clearly be seen. To fulfil her high vocation of intense union with God, Elizabeth needed the stability and regularity of the established community of Dijon; that would give her the environment she required.

As a final gesture, Elizabeth went and bought herself a new pair of gloves for her last dance, so that no one would suspect that she was to enter Carmel so soon. What did the price of pair of gloves matter, when her heart was already in the cloister that was to be her home.

Ready to take the plunge

Elizabeth had expressed to a friend her desire to suffer for love of Jesus, and the friend had replied, "God takes people like yourself at their word and accepts their self-giving."

With her lovely smile Elizabeth had replied, "I am ready to take the plunge. I hope I do suffer; that's what I'm entering Carmel for and if the good God overlooked me for a single day, I would think he had forgotten me."

Now that same friend was with her and her family as they attended Mass and Elizabeth prepared to go through the doors into Carmel's cloister. Their eyes met as they recalled that conversation. "I can't describe what I saw," she said later. "Her looks were almost angelic, no longer human. Her eyes were luminous, transparent; they shone with a heavenly light. I'll never forget the impression they made on me. That was the last time I saw her this side of Carmel's grills."

Into the Land of Carmel

Three days after her entrance into Carmel, the Prioress sent a photo of the community to the Lisieux Carmel, with Elizabeth in her postulant's dress in the front. A note attached said of their new postulant: "Sister Elizabeth of the Trinity, who will be a saint, for she already has a remarkable disposition for it".

Seeing her absorbed in prayer at supper that first evening, some of the older sisters thought, "that can't last", but it did. On entering her cell for the first time, with its white walls and simple furnishings, Elizabeth exclaimed, "God is here!"

Her cell was sparsely furnished; it contained a bed with a straw paillasse, a straw-seated chair and a writing desk. The floor was of bare boards. There was no heat or running water and the only light was from a small oil lamp. Above her bed was a large black wooden cross without the figure of Christ: the Carmelite was to put herself there. On the white walls were three sepia pictures with a small picture on the door that signified the sister's name. It was a simple room, but the very plainness and absence of superfluities gave it an austere beauty and a visual peace. Elizabeth described what it meant to her:

…it is filled with God and I spend such wonderful hours there alone with the Bridegroom. For me, the cell is something sacred, it is his intimate sanctuary, just for him and his little bride. We are so much 'together', I am silent, I listen to him…it is so good to hear everything he has to say. And I love him while I ply my needle and work on this dear serge which I have so longed to wear.[7]

A happy Carmelite

Guite and Elizabeth has been accustomed to making their own clothes, so Elizabeth was happy sewing in the quiet of her cell; she was also given the task of sweeping and dusting the choir and arranging fresh flowers for the altar, a task that delighted her because it brought her close to her Lord in the Blessed Sacrament. In such an atmosphere she began to blossom once more and her health began to improve. She was a happy Carmelite, Mother Germaine said, and that happiness came through when she described going to the wash for the first time. It was a back-breaking task, done by hand, with the sisters kneeling round the large tub:

> For the occasion I put on my nightcap, my brown dress all turned up, a large apron over that and, to complete the outfit, our wooden shoes. I went down like that to the laundry room where they were scrubbing for all they were worth, and I tried to do like the others. I splashed

and soaked myself all over, but that didn't matter, I was thrilled! Oh, you see, everything is delightful in Carmel, we find God at the wash just as at prayer. Everywhere there is only him. We live him, breathe him. If you knew how happy I am, my horizon grows larger each day.[8]

She entered fully into the atmosphere of Carmel, where God's love was the reason for being there:

The life of a Carmelite is a communion with God from morning till night and from night till morning. If he did not fill our cells and cloisters, how empty they would be! But we see him in every circumstance, for we bear him within us, and our life is an anticipation of heaven.[9]

Her intense love of silence often made her the butt of the sisters' teasing, and she was always ready to accept "silence challenges" from them, which of course she invariably won. Only charity came before silence for her.

Interior silence

Elizabeth realised that prayer was not only her response to God, but that interior silence was needed in order to allow God to speak. Desires, joys, fears and sorrows, the inner chatter of "self" make a continual noise within that so easily drowns out the "small still voice" of God. She wanted to bring a unity into her life that was wholly directed to living in God's presence, obeying Jesus' word to "seek first the kingdom of heaven and its righteousness".

Seeking the kingdom of heaven first is like a magnet that draws everything else into its rightful place. She wanted that "single eye" of which Jesus speaks, which allowed her more and more to see things through his eyes: "How necessary is this lovely inner unity to one who wants to live the life of heaven already here below!" It drew her into a "lovely simplicity":

> From now on the Master has complete freedom - he is free to flow out to her, to give himself without measure. And she, simplified, unified, becomes the throne of him who never changes, because unity is the throne of the Holy Trinity.[10]

When she had been accepted for the Dijon Carmel, she had hoped, because of her intense love for Jesus, that her name would be Elizabeth of Jesus, but, surely at the prompting of the Holy Spirit, the Prioress said that her name would be Elizabeth of the Trinity. Disappointed at first, Elizabeth began to ponder the depths of her prophetic "new name", and her life from then on would be an entering into the mystery of God himself. On her first Feast of the Trinity in Carmel, she wrote:

> Oh yes…this feast of the Three is really my own, for there is none like it. It was really nice in Carmel, for it is a feast of silence and adoration; I had never understood so well the Mystery and the whole vocation in my name.[11]

Her prayer was to enter into the "inner room" of which Jesus spoke, and she described what she found as "heaven":

> We possess our heaven within us, since he who satisfies the hunger of the glorified in the light of vision gives himself to us in faith and mystery, it is the Same One! It seems to me that I have found my heaven on earth, since God is heaven and God is in my soul.[12]

A continual delight

This continual sense of the Lord's presence remained with her strongly throughout her period of postulancy, making prayer a continual delight as well as a need. The community had no difficulty in accepting her for her clothing, and on 8th December, Feast of the Immaculate Conception, she at last received the brown Carmelite habit and white cloak she had so longed for.

The year would be a testing time for the community. In July 1901 Mother Mary of the Cross had led a small group of sisters to found the Carmel at Paray-le-Monial, and Mother Germaine of Jesus was elected Prioress of the Dijon Carmel on 9th October. In 1902, the Secular Government of France, under Émile Combes, had enacted the Law of Associations even more harshly, and closed down schools, convents and other institutions run by Catholic religious Orders, forcing many of them into exile. Although the Dijon Carmel had been assured they would not be affected, they did have to close their chapel to

Elizabeth of the Trinity

outside visitors for several months, and the threat of exile still hung over them.

Doubts and difficulties

For Elizabeth herself, as her year's novitiate began, her spiritual life underwent an abrupt change. She lost her sense of God's presence and all the joy and ease she had experienced in prayer. Her mind, imagination and feelings ran riot, leaving her in complete confusion and turmoil. Suddenly, the Lord who had been so close to her seemed beyond her reach. She even began to doubt her vocation.

Elizabeth could not understand what was happening to her and neither could her Prioress nor Fr Vallée, who had helped her so much in the past. He preached the community retreat in October, and emerged downcast from the parlour after speaking with Elizabeth. Over and over again he repeated to himself, "What have you done to my Elizabeth? You have changed her."

What was happening to her? Had something really gone wrong? There were probably various reasons for the change in her. Before she entered Carmel Elizabeth had kept a diary in which she recorded in meticulous detail her daily battle against her failings, her defeats and successes, in keeping herself in the presence of God. While God's grace was undoubtedly working powerfully in her in this, perhaps a great deal of her peace and recollection was due to her strong will suppressing such characteristics of her personality, such as her temper, her impetuousness, her desire for other to give in to her. But God's peace comes from a transformation of all aspects of the personality, bringing harmony without straining or forcing, although always co-operating with the grace of God.

Prayer is not always easy

Again, Elizabeth needed the trial presented by her loss of joy and the sense of God's presence and facility in prayer; she had a deeply contemplative spirit, and although she had had to struggle with her faults and failings she lacked real understanding of the difficulties of those less gifted in prayer than she was. She had to learn through hard and bitter experience that prayer is not always easy. This brought her to a deeper humility and a realisation of how completely her gifts were given to her by God.

However, during this difficult period God was accomplishing a truly positive work in her. He was calling her to enter into a deeper relationship, he was purifying the "oversensitivity" that Elizabeth had said was her besetting fault, so that she would cling to him whether she experienced his presence or not. She had to pass beyond feelings to settle her will only on the will of God. Elizabeth longed to love him with all her heart, but for this he had to increase her capacity to receive his love. His life is so infinite that it constantly comes up against the limit of human capacity to contain it, and suffering, darkness, the feeling of God's absence, is the way in which he quarries out those depths in order for the human heart to receive him. Thanks to Elizabeth's generosity of spirit, even though she did not understand what God was doing in her, she embraced him in the darkness and he was able to work his will in her. She had enough courage to reach out blindly for God in the darkness, even where she could not see, trusting him to lead her through safely. Afterwards she could look back and see how the Lord had been guiding and forming her, and use this deeper wisdom and insight to help others going through a similar experience, as this letter shows:

> It seems to me that God is asking for abandonment and unlimited trust during the painful times when you feel those terrible voids. Believe that at those times he is hollowing out in your soul capacities to receive him, capacities that are, in a way, as infinite as he himself. Try then to will to be wholly joyful under the hand that crucifies you.[13]

There were joys for her during this painful time. In the June of that year Mother Germaine had put her in contact with a newly ordained priest, Henri Beaubis, who was going out to China as a missionary. In a letter to him, Elizabeth wrote:

> Oh, how powerful over souls is the apostle who remains always at the Spring of living waters; then he can overflow without his soul ever becoming empty, since he lives in communion with the Infinite![14]

This was true for Henri, but it was equally true for Elizabeth herself, the apostolic contemplative. Only by remaining close to the source of grace could either of them be fruitful for souls.

Praying for priests

On 22nd July 1902 Guite announced her engagement to Georges Chevignard, a doctor, who like Guite was an accomplished musician. They were married three months later on the Feast of St Teresa of Avila, 15th October. This began a friendship between Elizabeth and George's brother André, a seminarian. St Teresa of Avila had founded her Carmels with the express intention of praying for priests, and this friendship increased Elizabeth's zeal for intercessory prayer. Teresa had expressly said that if her daughters' prayers and sacrifices were not apostolic, directed towards the salvation of souls, then they had mistaken their vocation. As she wrote in a letter to André:

> Staying by [this] source is like someone who is starving; and this is how I understand the Carmelite's apostolate as well as the priest's; they both can radiate God, give him to souls, if they constantly stay close to this divine source.[15]

Despite her inner difficulties, in December the Community had no difficulty in accepting her for her Profession, which took place on Epiphany Sunday, 11th January 1903.

The Praise of Glory

Although Elizabeth had a crisis of faith on the eve of her Profession, after making her Profession vows the former inner calm and peace returned. She was given the post of helping at the turn, that is, liaising with the extern sisters on the outside of the monastery who received visitors, dealt with workmen and other matters, while inside the monastery Elizabeth would deliver messages, bringing sisters to the parlour, and deal with supplies and deliveries. She was also made assistant in the office that made the habits for the sisters, which gave her the opportunity of those precious times of silence in her cell as she did her sewing.

Spiritually, she developed rapidly in union with God. She loved the times on Sundays and Feast days when the Blessed Sacrament would be exposed in the oratory. She spent as much time as her duties allowed in the choir, relishing those times of silent prayer and adoration. Before she entered Carmel, a friend, seeing her absorbed in prayer after Mass, had asked her what she prayed for. Elizabeth replied very simply that "we just love each other", and this, really, was the essence of her prayer.

She described the simplicity of this to a young friend of hers, Françoise de Sourdon:

You must build a little cell within your soul as I do. Remember that God is there and enter it from time to time; when you feel nervous or you're unhappy, quickly seek refuge there and tell the Master all about it. Ah, if you got to know him a little, prayer wouldn't bore you any more; to me it seems to be rest, relaxation. We come quite simply to the One we love, stay close to him like a little child in the arms of its mother, and we let our heart go.[16]

Entering into Jesus' own prayer

Sometimes Elizabeth did admit to times of dryness, when she felt tempted to get up and leave the choir, but her love and fidelity kept her there. In her prayer of love Jesus was leading her ever more deeply into his life. She described that what she was doing when she went to prayer was entering into Jesus' own prayer, and she was discovering the secret of this from her increasing love of the Scriptures, of the Gospel of St John, and even more from him whom she called "her beloved St Paul".

She entered into Jesus' intercessory prayer that continues unceasingly in heaven (*Heb* 7:25, 9:25). Just as Jesus has passed "through the veil" into heaven, so in her prayer Elizabeth, too, passed through the veil, seeing that "we bear him within us and our life is an anticipated heaven".

It was also the "spirit of sonship" that enabled her to call out as a child of God, with Jesus, "Abba" (*Rm* 8:15;

Ga 4:6). Then, it became as it always had with Elizabeth, a dialogue of love that entered into that love which is the inner life of the Holy Trinity; where the Father pours out his love on the Son, the Son replies with the whole of his love to the Father; this bond of eternal, unbroken love is the Holy Spirit, the love between the Father and the Son.

On their holidays beside the sea at Biarritz before her entry into Carmel, Elizabeth loved the power of the sea, and also its tranquillity, and she drew on this imagery in a letter to Canon Angles where she described that love which was almost overwhelming her:

> I feel so much love over my soul, it is like an Ocean I immerse and lose myself in; it is my vision on earth while awaiting the face-to-face vision in light. He is in me, I am in him. I have only to love him, to let myself be loved, all the time, through all things.[17]

Reading the writings of saints

Around this time Elizabeth was reading the writings of St John of the Cross and also studying St Paul. She discovered another dimension to her vocation when, around Christmas 1903 Sr Aimée directed her to Ephesians 3:16, where St Paul speaks of the Christian vocation of living to the "praise of his glory". Elizabeth first made mention of it in a letter to Abbé Chevignard in January 1904, where she showed how this letter to the Ephesians was giving her so much spiritual food.

Christ's "exceeding charity" was her vision on earth, which surpasses all understanding; she also reiterated her apostolic vocation of prayer, united with that of Christ:

Since Our Lord dwells in our souls, his prayer belongs to us, and I wish to live in communion with it unceasingly, keeping myself like a little vase at the Source, at the Fountain of life, so that later I can communicate it to souls by letting its floods of infinite charity overflow.[18]

Prayer to the Trinity

Later that year, on 21st November, the Feast of the Presentation of Our Lady in the Temple, Elizabeth, with the rest of the community, renewed her Profession vows, and afterwards went to her cell and composed her famous Prayer to the Trinity:

O my God, Trinity whom I adore, help me to be utterly forgetful of self so as to be rooted in you, as changeless and calm as if I were already in eternity. May nothing disturb my peace or draw me out of you, my unchangeable One, but at every moment may I penetrate ever more deeply into the depths of your mysteries: Make me peaceful, make me your heaven, a home you love and the place where you can be at rest; may I never leave you there alone, but be there entirely absorbed, in living faith, wholly adoring, freely given up to your creative action.

O my Christ, whom I love, crucified by love, I long to be the bride of your heart; I long to cover you with glory and love you…until I die of love. But I realise how weak I am and I beg you to clothe me with yourself, to identify my soul with the movements of your soul. Immerse yourself in me, possess me, substitute yourself for me, that my life becomes but a reflection of your life. Enter into me as Adorer, Restorer and Saviour.

Eternal Word, Utterance of my God, I want to spend my life listening to you. I want to make myself completely open to learn everything from you. Through all the nights, through every privation and weakness I want to be with you always, living beneath your blazing light, beloved Star; so fascinate me that I can no longer stray from your radiance.

Consuming Fire, Spirit of Love, come down upon me and make me as it were an incarnation of the Word; may I be another humanity in which he lives out once more his mystery. And you, Father, bend down to your poor little creature, cover her with your shadow and see in her only the Well-Beloved in whom you were well pleased.

O my "Three", my All, my Bliss, infinite Solitude, Immensity in which I lose myself, I give myself up to you as your prey; immerse yourself in me that I may be immersed in you until I go to gaze forever, in your light, on the boundless depths of your greatness.[19]

Spiritual journey

In this sublime prayer Elizabeth summed up her spiritual journey thus far. It is an extended meditation of the Annunciation to Mary in the context of the praying soul to which the retreat director, Fr Fages, OP in the community retreat from 12th-21st November 1904 had laid especial emphasis. Each of the Trinity's individual attributes is clearly defined: the Father "bends over" Elizabeth to envelop her in the Holy Spirit who will bring forth the likeness of Christ in her soul. She wants to be so like her Master that the Father will see in her only the likeness of his beloved Son. She wants to be fascinated by the rays of his radiance, so that she is unable to take her eyes from him. In an earlier letter to Abbé Chevignard, (Letter 158), she said that she wanted "'to be buried in God with Christ' to be lost in this Trinity who will one day be our vision, and in this divine light penetrate into the depth of the Mystery".

She struck another note in this prayer, that Christ was crucified by love, and she knew that she, too, must follow him in this. Her health had never been strong, and as early as 1903 she had been diagnosed as having Addison's disease, which left her increasingly weak, with such symptoms as loss of appetite, tiredness, anaemia and stomach disorders. She was finding the cold in the unheated Carmel difficult to bear over the winter months. She tried to carry on with her duties at the turn, following all the community activities, and when Lent 1905 began, hoped very much that she would be able to keep the Lenten fast with the rest of the community, but since she was having increased stomach pains and difficulty in eating, she was not allowed to. She revealed only later that she found it increasingly difficult to walk quickly when answering a call at the turn, and one day, when she was at the bottom of the stairs when the bell rang, had to make a real effort to climb even the first flight. When Mother Germaine asked her why she didn't have the simplicity to tell her how she was feeling, Elizabeth replied: "I just didn't think of it, Mother. In any case, the exceptions you were already making for me didn't make any difference, so I saw it as God's will for me." She was unable to have a good night's rest even when she was sent to bed early, so the exhaustion followed her day and night. She would spend the hour of silence before matins in the evening in the choir, pressed up close to the grille, to give her the courage and strength to keep her going through the Divine Office, until she struggled back to her cell and an uncomfortable night.

Joys during difficult times

There were joys for her that year, 19th April 1905, when Guite gave birth to her second child, Odette. Her first child, whom they called Elizabeth after her aunt, had been born on 11th March the previous year. She would eventually follow her aunt into the Dijon Carmel. Elizabeth's letters at this time were full of the delight she had in seeing the little babies. Then on 29th June, André Chevignard was ordained. It helped to offset the dryness and sense of God's absence that beset her at this time, perhaps at least partly due to her failing health.

Through the long summer months Elizabeth kept going, with her doctors prescribing rest and fresh air. Mother Germaine made sure she was out in the garden as much as possible and in the middle of August relieved her of duties at the turn; Elizabeth carried on with her sewing in the tranquillity of the garden, seeing it almost as a sort of retreat. During this time she also wrote her two treatises, "Heaven in Faith", and "Last Retreat". She went into her retreat proper on 8th October. She wrote to Abbé Chevignard asking for his prayers. For the first time she wrote about being "a sacrifice to the praise of his glory", because she wanted all her aspirations, all her actions, to be a homage to God. She felt that she was going on a divine journey, and indeed the community felt that she had "passed into God" and lived now on a higher plane. They noticed, too, that the Divine Office and other vocal prayers, which had sometimes proved a "distraction" to her intense inner recollection, had now become assimilated into her prayer, as an external expression of her desire to be a praise of glory.

Living heaven on earth

As for Elizabeth, she felt at the same time that she had
not reached the heights she yearned for, and yet that she
could not long remain at the height she had attained, and
asked to die young - a premonition she had had for many
years. At the end of November she wrote again to Abbé
Chevignard, using for the first time the Latin, though using
the nominative: "Laudem Gloriae" for "Praise of Glory",
which she felt expressed more completely the new stage in
her union with God.

What did she understand about being a "Praise of
Glory"? Many times she had reiterated her sense of living
heaven on earth in Carmel, and that life here was heaven
begun and ever in progress. Now, she understood that what
her vocation would be in heaven was already beginning
on earth.

In the "Last Retreat" Elizabeth spelt out in detail what
it meant:

A praise of glory is a soul that lives in God, that loves
him beyond all his gifts.

A praise of glory is a soul of silence that remains like
a lyre under the mysterious touch of the Holy Spirit, and
suffering is a string that produces still more beautiful
sounds.

A praise of glory is a soul that gazes on God in faith
and simplicity, that reflects all that he is.

A praise of glory is one who is always giving thanks. Each of her acts, her movements, her thoughts, her aspirations, at the same time that they are rooting her more deeply in love, are like an eternal sanctus.

In the heaven of her soul, the praise of glory has already begun her work of eternity. Her song is uninterrupted. She has wholly passed into praise and love.[20]

This was the inner life of Elizabeth of the Trinity as she passed into the final phase of her life and her climb up her personal calvary.

The Fellowship of his Sufferings

On Christmas Eve 1905, as Elizabeth was helping the other novices to prepare the crib, she was heard to murmur, "My little King of Love; we'll be very much closer to each other next year!"

Divining correctly that by this Elizabeth meant that she would be in heaven, her companion asked her, startled, "How do you know that?" Elizabeth looked at her, gave her usual radiant smile, but said nothing.

On New Year's Day it was the custom for the sisters to draw tickets with the name of their patron for that year. Elizabeth drew that of St Joseph, patron of a happy death. "He is coming to take me to the Father," she exclaimed in delight, and dismissed with a slight gesture the laughing and somewhat alarmed denials of her sisters who did not realise how seriously ill she was.

On Epiphany Sunday she should have moved out of the novitiate into the fully professed community, but Mother Germaine asked her to remain in the novitiate to help with the new postulants who had recently entered. Elizabeth had often been given as their "angel" to new entrants, a sister who helped them adapt to and learn about their new life.

The road she would tread

The first three months of the year were very difficult for Elizabeth as she tried to cope with her increasing pain and exhaustion, and at the beginning of March she turned once more to her beloved St Paul to give her guidance. There, she found the words "communion with his suffering and conformity with his death" in Philippians 3:10, and knew that this was the road she would tread.

Her premonition about St Joseph being the patron of a happy death seemed to be correct, because leading up to his Feast Elizabeth was finding it impossible to eat and the full extent of her illness became evident. Only then was her family told of the severity of her illness, which her mother accepted with deep acceptance of the will of God.

On St Joseph's Feast, 19th March, she became seriously ill and the following day she was moved into the infirmary. She was given the anointing of the sick and remained ill through Holy Week, but by Easter she had recovered somewhat. Three doctors came to examine her and the possibility of an operation was discussed and rejected. For Elizabeth, this was a relief, because she wanted to remain in her beloved cloister.

Visits from family

From now on, all restrictions on letter writing were lifted, and the family came to visit her roughly once a fortnight now. In July, Mother Mary of Jesus returned from Paray-le-Monial to Dijon on business, and wrote back to her community:

> I have had a beautiful sermon coming into contact with Sister Elizabeth of the Trinity. The little sister is a real saint; she speaks of her approaching death with a lovely simplicity, a joyous serenity and peace, and lives in the anticipation of seeing God, in perfect surrender and love. She seems to be already in the retreat of eternity.[21]

Elizabeth asked for a statue of Our Lady that she had had while at home, and although it was almost too heavy for her to carry, it went with her everywhere; she called it "Janua Caeli", gate of heaven. She loved spending her time in prayer in the infirmary tribune, a small upstairs room from which she could see the Blessed Sacrament. When the sisters saw the statue outside, they knew that "Laudem Gloriae" was there.

A deep inner joy

Even in the midst of her suffering she retained a deep inner joy and peace. In June she wrote to Canon Angles, referring to the times when she had seemed close to death:

> Since I wrote to you last, heaven seemed to be open again, and you prayed so hard that I am still captive; but a happy captive who, in the depths of her soul, sings night and day of the love of her Master, he is so good

… You would think he had only me to love and think about from the way he gives himself to my soul, but this is so I, in return, might surrender myself to him for his Church and all his interests, so I might care for his honour like my holy Mother Teresa.[22]

By August Elizabeth had become extremely weak and emaciated due to the severe inflammation of her stomach and a scorching thirst; almost the only thing she could eat was small pieces of chocolate, Bruges bread or cottage cheese. The Carmelite habit became too heavy for her to wear, so her mother brought her material from which a lighter and warmer habit could be made. Mme Catez worried that with the approach of autumn and colder weather she might suffer from the cold, but Elizabeth assured her that there was a stove in the infirmary. She was delaying remaining there, for the moment, because it would mean she could no longer visit her beloved tribune where there was no heat.

Delicate love

Leading up to St Teresa of Avila's Feast day, 15th October, the community also celebrated the beatification of the Carmelite martyrs of Compiegne. Guite and Georges provided the music, and Fr Vallée gave talks for three days. He saw Elizabeth for the last time in the parlour, and later wrote to Mme Catez that Elizabeth's last days were "so uncommonly, so divinely beautiful".

The following week the clothing ceremony took place of a young lay sister, Marie Joseph. By this time Elizabeth's body was almost skeletal, but she insisted on sewing the white veil for the sister, even though she was almost too weak to hold the needle. It was just one way in which she could show her love for her sister, the delicate love she had shown to all the community through her time with them.

Around this time a visiting priest gave her Holy Communion and found it a harrowing experience, writing to Mme Catez:

> I'll never forget the impression your angelic daughter made on me when I gave her Holy Communion three weeks before she died. I had been warned, but when I saw her tongue red as if on fire I was so unnerved that my hand was trembling as I laid the sacred Host on it. I considered it one of the greatest graces of my priestly ministry given me by the Sacred Heart that I was able to bring her the consolation of Holy Communion when she was so soon to be crowned in heaven. Our Lord seemed to want me to understand that the love which burned in this holy victim was far more fiery than the fire that was consuming her body.[23]

Tranquillity lying deep within

Sometimes her physical agony almost overwhelmed her. She saw her Prioress as a priest offering her to God on the altar of her suffering:

My beloved priest, your little victim is suffering very, very much, it is a kind of physical agony. She feels so cowardly, cowardly enough to scream! But the Being who is the Fullness of Love visits her, keeps her company, makes her enter into communion with him, while he makes her understand that as long as he leaves her on earth, he will measure out suffering to her. [24]

Beneath all her agony, there was still a peace, joy and tranquillity that lay deep within her. One day, when she was showing the same serenity as usual and speaking of her happiness, just as Mother Germaine was leaving the infirmary, Elizabeth pointed to the open window close to her bed, saying, "Mother, are you at peace leaving me all alone like this?" Mother Germaine didn't understand what she meant, and Elizabeth added, "I'm suffering so much that I now understand suicide. But be at peace: God is there and he protects me."

Nevertheless, there were times when heaven opened to her a foretaste of what would be. One morning Mother Germaine came to her and Elizabeth exclaimed:

Mother, a little more and you wouldn't have found Laudem Gloriae on earth any more! Yesterday evening I felt as if I was suffering a complete collapse, when all of a sudden I felt as if I was being invaded by Love. It's impossible to describe what I experienced; it was a fire of infinite sweetness and at the same time I felt it wounding me mortally. I believe if it had lasted much longer I would have died.[25]

The secret of her serenity in the face of atrocious suffering lay in a remark she made to her mother, writing to her at the end of September:

> I cannot say I love suffering in itself, but I love it because it conforms me to him who is my Bridegroom and my Love. Oh, you see, that bestows such sweet peace, and profound joy on the soul, and you end up putting your happiness in everything that is irritating.[26]

She was able to see her family in the parlour for the last time on 29th October, and it was the last time she was able to leave the infirmary.

Last days

Her joy remained even when she felt a sense of abandonment, remarking to a sister of her impending death, "I'll go in pure faith and I like that much better. I'll be even more like my Master and it will be more real." She received Holy Communion for the last time on the Feast of All Saints, when in her joy she thought that the bells ringing in honour of the Feast were for her, but she had a few more days yet on earth. Her sisters were struck by the fact that even with a high fever, a headache so severe they thought she might contract meningitis, her mind was still lucid. She had once written that she was "Elizabeth of the Trinity, that is, Elizabeth disappearing, losing herself, letting herself be invaded by the 'Three'" and now it seemed her wish was granted; as a sister remarked, she no longer prayed, she had become prayer, and also resembled the Man of Sorrows.

Longing for heaven

One evening, Sr Agnes of Jesus, seeing her in agony, said to her, "My poor little sister, you can't bear any more, can you?"

"No, I can't bear any more".

"You long for heaven, don't you?"

"Yes. Until now I have surrendered myself to him, but I'm his bride and I have the right to say to him, 'Let us go!' We love each other so much, I'm longing to see him. Oh, I love him so much!"

Her final night on earth was extremely painful, but towards dawn her sufferings eased somewhat and she became calmer. As she lay on her bed, now silent and peaceful, her sisters came and knelt round her bed as the first Angelus bell began to ring. Elizabeth lay on her right side, her head thrown back slightly, her eyes wide open now, fixed on a point just over the heads of her sisters, in ecstasy rather than in agony. Her face was wonderfully beautiful, and the sisters could not take their eyes off her. It seemed as if she was already looking at heaven.

About 6.15 a.m., on 9th November 1906, still with that radiant expression, she died so peacefully that they couldn't be sure of the exact moment. She had lived heaven on earth and slipped away so easily into its fullness. Her last words were: "I am going to Light to Love to Life!"

Her mission in heaven

After her death, Mother Germaine found an envelope addressed to herself, Elizabeth's last message to her. During those last months, the teacher had become the pupil as Elizabeth progressed to the heights of union with God. She understood her Prioress' sense of her inadequacies and sought to encourage her. Mother Germaine had been her "priest" offering her on the altar of her pain, and now Elizabeth would be her "priest" looking over her, writing:

> "You are uncommonly loved," loved by that love of preference that the Master had here below for some and which brought them so far. He does not say to you as to Peter, "Do you love me more than these?" Mother, listen to what he tells you: "Let yourself be loved more than these! That is, without fearing that any obstacle will be a hindrance to it, for I am free to pour out my love on whom I wish! Let yourself be loved more than these" is your vocation.[27]

A few weeks before her death Elizabeth wrote a note to Sr Marie-Odile, who had gone with the foundation to Paray-le-Monial. In it, she expressed what her mission would be in heaven:

> I think that in heaven my mission will be to draw souls by helping them to go out of themselves to cling to God by a wholly simple and loving movement, and to keep them in this great silence within that will allow God to communicate himself to them and transform them into himself.[28]

Elizabeth's mission is to guide souls on the path of prayer, a path that is simple, because it is to allow oneself to be loved by God and to love him in return with the love that he himself pours into the heart. And the very simplicity of this will allow the soul to reach the heights of holiness and union with God that Elizabeth herself attained. In her letter to her Prioress she wrote:

> I bequeath to you this vocation which was mine in the heart of the Church Militant and which from now on I will unceasingly fulfil in the Church Triumphant: The Praise of Glory of the Holy Trinity.[29]

From the Writings of
Saint Elizabeth of the Trinity

Elizabeth attended a retreat given by Fr Hoppentot SJ, in January 1900, and afterwards wrote this prayer:

> Jesus, my Beloved, how wonderful it is to love you, to belong to you, to have you for my All! Now that you are coming every day to me, may our union be even closer. May my life be a continual prayer, a long act of love. May nothing whatever distract me from you, no noise or distractions. I would so love, my Master, to live with you in silence. But what I love most of all is to do your will, and since you want me to be in the world at present, I submit myself with all my heart for love of you.
>
> I offer the cell of my heart to be your little Bethany; come and live there, I love you so much…I would like to console you and I offer myself to you as a victim, Master, for you, with you. I accept in advance every sacrifice, every trial, even that of no longer feeling you with me. I ask only one thing: always to be generous and faithful, always; I never want to take it back. I want to do your will perfectly, to respond always to your grace; I long to be a saint with you and for you, but

I realise my weakness - be you my sanctity. If I ever take it back, I beg you, I plead with you: while I am yours, let me die. I am your 'little spoilt pet', you tell me, but soon perhaps trials will come and then it will be me who will give to you. Master, it isn't the gifts, the consolations you pour out on me that I'm looking for, it is you and you alone! Watch over me always, make me more and more your own, may everything in me belong to you: break, cut away, all that displeases you that I may be all yours. Each heartbeat of mine is an act of love. My Jesus, my God, how good it is to love you, to be totally yours![30]

My heaven was beginning on earth

On 15th July 1903 Elizabeth wrote to Canon Angles after her Profession, describing her inner life as a professed Carmelite:

How many things have happened since my last letter! I heard the Church say, "Veni Sponsa Christi"; she consecrated me, and now all is "consummated". Rather, everything is beginning, for profession is only a dawn; and each day my "life as a bride" seems to me more beautiful, more luminous, more enveloped in peace and love. During the night that preceded the great day, while I was in choir awaiting the Bridegroom, I understood that my heaven was beginning on earth; heaven in faith, with suffering and immolation for him whom I love!... I think that in Carmel it is so simple to live by love; from morning to evening the Rule is there to express the will of God, moment by moment. ...since he is always with me, prayer, the heart-to-heart, must never end! I feel him so alive in my soul. I have only to recollect myself to find him within me, and that is my whole happiness. He has placed in my heart a thirst for the infinite and such a great need for love that he alone can satisfy it. Oh, go to him like a little child to its mother so he may fill, invade, everything, and then take me and carry me away in his arms. I think we must be so simple with God![31]

Be wholly joyful under the hand which crucified you

Canon Angles' mother had been deeply traumatised during an operation when the anaesthetic was insufficient to make her completely unconscious during an operation. Elizabeth wrote her this letter to help and encourage her. She drew on her own increasing illness and the way in which she was dealing with her own suffering:

If you knew how attached my soul is to yours, I would even say how 'ambitious' I am for it! I would like it to be wholly surrendered, wholly adhering to that God who loves it with so great a love!...I believe that the secret of peace and happiness is to forget oneself, not be preoccupied with oneself. That doesn't mean not feeling one's physical or mental sufferings; the saints themselves passed through these crucifying states, but they did not dwell on them; they continually left these things behind them; when they felt themselves affected by them, they were not surprised, for they knew "they were but dust", as the Psalmist sings; but he also adds, "With God's help, I will be unblemished, and I will guard myself from the depths of sinfulness within me"…since you allow me to speak to you like a beloved sister, it seems to me that God is asking you for abandonment and unlimited trust during the painful times when you feel these terrible voids. Believe that at those times he is hollowing out in your soul capacities to receive him, capacities that are, in a way, as infinite as he himself. Try then to be wholly joyful under the hand that crucifies you; I would even say that you should look at each suffering, each trial, as "a proof of love" that comes to you directly from God in order to unite you to him.

Forgetting yourself with respect to your health does not mean neglecting to take care of yourself, for that is your duty and the best of penances, but do it with great abandonment, saying "thank you" to God no matter what happens. When your soul is burdened and fatigued by the weight of your body, do not be discouraged, rather go by faith and love to him who said: "Come to me and

I will refresh you". As for your spirit, never let yourself be depressed by the thought of your sufferings. The great St Paul says, "Where sin abounds, grace abounds all the more". It seems to me the weakest, even the guiltiest, soul that is the one that has the most reason for hope; and the act of forgetting self and throwing oneself into the arms of God glorifies him and gives him more joy than all the turning inward and all the self-examinations that make one live with one's own infirmities, though the soul possesses in its very centre a Saviour who wants at every moment to purify it.

Do you remember that beautiful passage where Jesus says to his Father "that he has given him power over all flesh so that he might give eternal life to it"? That is what he wants to do in you; at every moment, he wants you to go out of yourself, to leave all preoccupations, in order to withdraw into the solitude he has chosen for himself in the depths of your heart. *He* is always there, although you don't feel it; he is waiting for you and wants to establish a "wonderful communion" with you, as we sing in the beautiful liturgy, an intimacy between bride and bridegroom; he, through this continual contact, can deliver you from your weaknesses, your faults, from all that troubles you. Didn't he say: "I have come not to judge but to save". *Nothing* should keep you from going to him. Don't pay too much attention to whether you are fervent or discouraged; it is the law of our exile to pass from one state to the other like that. Believe that *he* never changes, that in his goodness he is always bending over you to carry you away and keep you safe in him. If, despite everything, emptiness and sadness overwhelm you, unite this agony with that of the Master in the Garden of Olives, when he said to his Father: "If it is possible, let this cup pass me by". …it may perhaps seem difficult to forget yourself. Do not worry about it; if you knew how simple it is…I am going to give you my 'secret': think about this God who dwells within you, whose temple you are; Saint Paul speaks like this and we can believe him. Little by little, the soul gets used to living in his sweet company, it understands that it is carrying within it a little heaven where the God of love has fixed his home. Then it is as if it breathes a divine atmosphere; I would even say that only its body still lives on earth, while the soul lives beyond the clouds and the veils, in him who is the Unchanging One. Do not say that this is not for you, that you are too wretched; on the contrary, that is only one more reason for going to him who saves. We will be purified, not by looking at this wretchedness, but by looking at him who is all purity and holiness. Saint Paul says that "He has predestined us to be conformed to his image". In the saddest times, think that the divine artist is using his chisel to make his work more beautiful, and remain at peace beneath the hand that is working on you.[32]

Lost in God

Elizabeth saw in Mary the model of the contemplative, prayerful soul. In the latter part of August 1906 she wrote two treatises, "Heaven in Faith" and "Last Retreat", and in them gave a beautiful exposition on Mary:

> "If you knew the gift of God"… There is one who knew this gift of God, one who did not lose a particle of it, one who was so pure and luminous that she seemed to be the Light itself. "Speculum Justitiae". One whose life was so simple, so lost in God that there is hardly anything we can say about it.
>
> "Virgo Fidelis"; that is, Faithful Virgin, "who kept all these things in her heart". She remained so little, so recollected in God's presence, in the seclusion of the temple, that she drew down upon herself the delight of the Holy Trinity: "Because he has looked upon the lowliness of his servant, henceforth all generations shall call me blessed". The Father, bending down to this beautiful creature, who was so unaware of her own beauty, willed that she be the Mother in time of him whose Father he is in eternity. Then the Spirit of love who presides over all of God's works came upon her; the Virgin said her *fiat*: "Behold the servant of the Lord, be it done to me according to your word". And the greatest of mysteries was accomplished. By the descent of the Word in her, Mary became forever God's prey.

It seems to me that the attitude of the Virgin during the months that elapsed between the Annunciation and the Nativity is the model for interior souls, those who God has chosen to live within, in the depths of the bottomless abyss. In what peace, in what recollection Mary lent herself to everything she did! How even the most trivial things were divinised by her! For through it all the Virgin remained the adorer of the gift of God! This did not prevent her from spending herself outwardly when it was a matter of charity; the Gospel tells us that Mary went in haste to the mountains of Judea to visit her cousin Elizabeth. Never did the ineffable vision that she contemplated within herself in any way diminish her outward charity.[33]

He in us, we in him

From the age of seven, when she began to go to Sunday Mass regularly with her mother, Elizabeth had an intense hunger for Christ in Holy Communion and loved the many hours she spent in adoration before the Blessed Sacrament. She expressed that love in a letter to Abbé Chevignard, which illustrated the way it nourished her charism of silence, praise and adoration.

It seems to me that nothing expresses the love in God's Heart than the Eucharist; it is union, consummation, he in us, we in him, and isn't that heaven on earth?

Heaven in faith while awaiting the face-to-face vision we so desire. Then "we will be satisfied when his glory appears," when we see him in his light. Don't you find that the thought of this meeting refreshes the soul, this talk with him whom it loves solely? Then everything disappears and it seems that one is already entering into the mystery of God!...

This whole mystery is so much "ours," as you said to me in your letter. Oh! pray, won't you, that I may live fully my bridal dowry. That I may be wholly available, wholly vigilant in faith, so the Master can bear me wherever he wishes. I wish to stay always close to him, who knows the whole mystery, to hear everything from him. "The language of the Word is the infusion of the gift," oh yes, it is really so isn't it, that he speaks to our soul in silence. I find this dear silence a blessing. From Ascension to Pentecost, we were in retreat in the Cenacle, waiting for the Holy Spirit, and it was so good. During that whole Octave we have the Blessed Sacrament exposed in the oratory; those are divine hours spent in this little corner of heaven where we possess the vision in substance under the humble Host. Yes, he whom the blessed contemplate in light and we adore in faith is really the same One. The other day someone wrote to me such a beautiful thought, I send it on to you: "Faith is the face-to-face in darkness." Why wouldn't it be so for us, since God is in us and since he asks only to take possession of us as he took possession of the saints? Only, they were always attentive, as Père Vallée says: "They are silent, recollected, and their only activity is to be the being who receives." Let us unite ourselves, therefore, Father, in making happy him who "has loved us exceedingly" as St Paul says. Let us make a dwelling for him in our soul that is wholly at peace, in which the canticle of love, of thanksgiving, is always being sung; and then that great silence, the echo of the silence that is in God!...Then as you said, let us approach the all-pure, all-luminous Virgin, that she may present us to him whom she has penetrated so profoundly, and may our life be a continual communion, a wholly simple movement toward God.[34]

The freest soul

One of the friends Elizabeth had lovingly guided over the years was Françoise de Sourdon, whom she nicknamed "Framboise", Raspberry. High spirited and sometimes wilful, Framboise was now nineteen, and at the beginning of September 1906 Elizabeth wrote a last letter to her, which she jokingly referred to as a treatise. Entitled "The Greatness of our Vocation", it was indeed long, and Elizabeth wrote it in pencil, too weak now to hold a pen. She began to speak of pride and humility and how to seek the one thing necessary:

It seems to me the soul that is aware of its greatness enters into that "holy freedom of the children of God" of which the Apostle speaks, that is, it transcends all things, including self. The freest soul, I think, is the one most forgetful of self. If anyone were to ask me the secret of happiness I would say it is no longer to think of self, to deny oneself always. That is a good way to kill pride: let it starve to death! You see, pride is love of ourselves; well, love of God must be so strong that it extinguishes all our self-love. St Augustine says we have two cities within us, the city of God and the city of SELF. To the extent that the first increases, the second will be destroyed. A soul that lives by faith in God's presence, that has this "single eye" that Christ speaks of in the Gospel, that is, a purity of "intention" that seeks only God; this soul, it seems to me, would also live in humility: it would recognise his gifts to it - for "humility is truth" - but it would attribute nothing to itself, referring all to God as the Blessed Virgin did.

Be *strengthened in faith*, that is, never act except in the great light of God, never according to the impressions of your imagination. Believe that he loves you, that he wants to help you in the struggles you have to undergo. Believe in his love, his *exceeding* love, as St Paul says. Nourish your soul on the great thoughts of faith which will reveal to you all its richness and the end for which God has created you! If you live like this, your piety will never be a nervous exaltation as you fear but will be *true*. Truth is so beautiful, the truth of love. 'He loved me and gave himself up for me." That, my little child, is what it means to be true.

And finally, *grow in thanksgiving*. That is the last word of the programme and is but the consequence of it. If you walk rooted in Christ, strengthened in your faith, you will live in thanksgiving: the love of the sons of God! I wonder how a soul that has sounded the depths of love the Heart of God has *'for it'* could be anything but joyful in every suffering and sorrow.[35]

Overflowing with love

Elizabeth wrote this letter to Mme de Bobet, a family friend. Even at the end of her life her love flowed freely to her friends and family. She knew that what she had learnt of prayer and union with God is equally applicable to those who follow the Gospel in the world. It reads almost like a last will and testament echoing Jesus at the Last Supper, as her own life drew to an end:

The hour is drawing near when I am going to pass from this world to my Father, and before leaving I want to send you a note from my heart, a testament from my soul. Never was the Heart of the Master so overflowing with love as at the supreme moment when he was going to leave his own! It seems to me as if something similar is happening to his little bride at the evening of her life, and I feel as if a wave were rising from my heart to yours!...

I leave you my faith in the presence of God, of the God who is all love dwelling in our souls. I confide to you: it is this intimacy with him "within" that has been the beautiful sun illuminating my life, making it already an anticipated heaven. I do not fear my weakness; that is what gives me confidence. For the Strong One is within me and his power is almighty. It is able to do, says the Apostle, abundantly more than we can hope for![36]

Suggested Further Reading

Elizabeth of the Trinity, *I Have Found God: The Complete Works Volume 1*, edited by Conrad de Meester, translated by Alethia Kane, (Washington DC, ICS Publications, 1984).

Elizabeth of the Trinity, *I Have Found God: The Complete Works Volume 2*, edited by Conrad de Meester, translated by Alethia Kane, (Washington DC, ICS Publications, 1995).

Larkin, Thomas, *Elizabeth of the Trinity: Her Life and Spirituality*, (Dublin: Carmelite Centre of Spirituality, 1984).

Moorcroft, Jennifer, *He is my Heaven*, (Washington DC, ICS Publications, 2001).

Mosley, Joanne, *Elizabeth of the Trinity*, (Oxford, Teresian Press, 2012), two volumes.

Murphy, Marion T., OCD, *Always Believe in Love*, (New York, New York City Press, 2009).

Murphy, Marion T., OCD, *Elizabeth of the Trinity, Her Life and Spirituality*, (Leomister, Gracewing, 2011).

Philipon, M. M., *The Spiritual Doctrine of Elizabeth of the Trinity*, translated by a Benedictine of Stanbrook Abbey, (Washington DC, Teresian Charism Press, 1985).

The Praise of Glory: Translated by the Benedictines of Stanbrook Abbey, (London, Burns Oates & Washbourne Ltd, 1913).

Von Balthasar, Hans, *Two Sisters in the Spirit*, (San Francisco, Ignatius Press, 1970).

Endnotes

[1] Erroneously: a closer translation is 'God has sworn an oath' or 'God has made a promise'.

[2] Elizabeth de la Trinité, *J'ai Trouvé Dieu, Oevres Complètes, Tome 1b* (Paris, Editions du Cerf, 1980), p. 13.

[3] Elizabeth de la Trinité, *J'ai Trouvé Dieu, Oevres Complètes, Tome 11* (Paris, Editions du Cerf, 1979), Letter 14, p. 157.

[4] *Ibid.,* Letter 13, p. 155.

[5] *Ibid.,* Diary 105, p 77.

[6] Carmel de Dijon, *Soeur Elizabeth de la Trinité: Souvenirs* (Paris, Editions St Paul, 1945), p. 75.

[7] Elizabeth of the Trinity, *The Complete Works, Volume 2,* (Washington DC, ICS Publications, 1995), Letter 168, p. 108.

[8] *Ibid.,* Letter 89, p.16ff.

[9] *Ibid.,* Letter 123, p. 52.

[10] Elizabeth of the Trinity, *The Complete Works, Volume 1,* (Washington DC, ICS Publications, 1984), p. 143.

[11] Elizabeth of the Trinity, *The Complete Works, Volume 2,* (Washington DC, ICS Publications, 1995), Letter 113, p. 45.

[12] *Ibid.,* Letter 122, p. 51.

[13] *Ibid.,* Letter 249, p. 229.

[14] *Ibid.,* Letter 124, p. 53.

[15] *Ibid.,* Letter 158, p. 96.

[16] *Ibid.,* Letter 123, p. 52.

[17] *Ibid.,* Letter 177, p. 123.

[18] *Ibid.,* Letter 191, p. 144.

[19] *The Complete Works, Volume 1,* p. 183.

[20] *Ibid., vid.* p. 112.

[21] *Carmelite of the Sacred Heart*, p. 144.

[22] *The Complete Works, Volume 2*, Letter 275, p. 274.

[23] *Souvenirs*, pp. 247ff.

[24] *The Complete Works, Volume 1*, Letter 329, p. 353.

[25] *Souvenirs*, p. 248.

[26] *The Complete Works, Volume 2*, Letter 317, p. 338.

[27] *The Complete Works, Volume 1*, p. 179.

[28] *The Complete Works, Volume 2*, Letter 335, p. 360.

[29] *The Complete Works, Volume 1*, p. 180.

[30] *Oeuvres Complètes, Tome 11*, In 5 pp. 114ff.

[31] *The Complete Works, Volume 2*, Letter 169, pp. 110ff.

[32] *Ibid.*, Letter 249, pp. 228ff.

[33] *The Complete Works, Volume 1*, "Heaven in Faith" pp. 110ff. See also "Last Retreat" pp. 160ff.

[34] *The Complete Works, Volume 2*, Letter 165 pp. 106ff.

[35] *The Complete Works, Volume 1*, pp. 125ff.

[36] *The Complete Works, Volume 2*, Letter 333, p. 358.